A Bui ad

by

Malcolm Gedney

People

Roy Watson

John Housely

Ron Housely

Herbert Housely

Hazel (sister)

Joy (sister)

Geoff (brother)

Maurice Brickles

June Brickles

Jennifer Brickles

Brenda Brickles

Alec Brickles

Elsie Brickles

Belvoir Castle Estate was my first home. It was very posh, just like the rooms in the castle — old stone house, thick walls, low doorway, earth floor, outside toilet. Those that visited the castle lived a life of luxury, and there are plenty of tales about the parties held there and who visited it.

We later moved to a much better home the other side of Grantham when my father had to change jobs to work in a factory in town. The house was one of six next to a farm. I spent a lot of time with his two sons in their thirties in the fields at lambing season.

A recent photograph of home

Then along came my first encounter of this war. Out in the fields we spotted a barrage balloon rising into the sky very slowly with an object tangled in the cable. On closer inspection we realised it was a human being caught up. No way could they pull it down; it would have cut him in half. After a short while we heard a bang and the balloon fell to the ground. Later on, we heard they had caught him in a net, alive.

I was going to a small school half a mile away. I was enjoying my time there and doing very well at maths and other subjects. Then along came 1939, the war, and a very hard winter — snow so deep not a person could walk to the village. It was piled so high it was six weeks before some men were finally able to dig a way through and we could get to school and start learning again.

Me, grandfather, brother Geoff and grandmother

Later we walked to a village called Ancaster, five miles north, where my mother was born and went to school. There, my grandmother was very ill in bed. We met my two uncles there. They were on compassionate leave from the Navy. We went upstairs to see her. I stood by looking at her, one glance back and she died in front of me. Not a very nice thing to see.

The two younger brothers volunteered for the Navy, serving on mine disposals. One was lucky to survive one day when a mine washed up on the beach. He had gone back to fetch a tool when the mine blew up, killing his gang. The other brother was on mine sweepers. At least two of his ships sank under him but he lived to tell the tale.

The remaining four brothers never saw the war. My dad, however, was in the RAF, driving petrol tankers in France and Germany. When him and a pal were forced to make for an air raid shelter during a bombing raid, a bomb landed on its roof. From then on, Dad had fits which lasted until he died at the age of sixty-four. He was banned from driving and not allowed to use any machinery at work. That meant less money to bring home to feed us.

My parents Margaret and Freddy

While Dad was in the RAF, Mum and the family moved back to Ancaster to live with her dad and only sister. I was not accepted at the local school for a long time. Finally, after many months, they let me in the juniors the five-yearolds. I was about nine at the time and felt very embarrassed and angry.

But on the good side we had cousins across the road from us and others very near. That meant we had plenty of friends all going to the same school, which was about half a mile away. There was always a race there and back.

Time passed and I was eventually moved into another class. Having no interest in learning, sport was my thing football in the winter, cricket in the summer. Come holiday, my mother would take the four of us — me, my brother and two sisters — up a steep hill pushing a pram about four miles to a small village called Aisby where my grandparents and other relatives lived. As well as the usual games, we also went rabbiting on a farm at harvest time with Grandad and his dog. When the holidays were over, Mum would fetch us back the same way.

Miles Master

Then things really started to happen. Airfields, such as Cranwell, were all around and pilots were trained there. The types of planes used for the training were Miles Masters. The sky was full of them.

Time came to explore the countryside's fields and hedgerows of nesting birds. I made my own bow and arrows using crab apples as targets in trees. Every day at school I couldn't wait to get home and start enjoying life, practising with my bow and arrows or a catapult, shooting at some target. One time I made my own pipe, filled it with cigarette butts and gave it to my brother to try and make him sick! He has smoked all his life and is still doing so. I have never smoked. I then wandered further afield climbing trees of all sizes and getting in trouble, mostly with the local farmers but occasionally also the local bobby from the next village. He turned out to be both friend and foe. One of our games in the autumn was hide and seek, in and around a large shed with old rusty farm machinery. We shouldn't have been there and one night we got caught by our friend, the bobby. He cornered Ron and me and banged our heads together. It didn't hurt, we accepted it and that was that. School, as usual, was always waiting for us the next morning.

Then along came another episode — a Miles Master crashed about a quarter of a mile from our house. We were there like a shot but couldn't do a thing about the poor pilot, who may still have been alive, being burnt in his cockpit. A horrible sight. Going back to the good times out in the fields, birds nesting and football, all after school or weekends. Along came a new teacher, a man. After a while he planned and organised a proper football pitch. I didn't know about this until later, after my mates and I found an old motorbike and sidecar hidden in a cellar. The engine wouldn't work so we pushed it up a hill and rode down on it. No brakes! The teacher, though, had got to know about it and one day we pushed it up this hill and turned into a lane towards a farm where the father of a lad from our class worked. We loaded lengths of long timber on the sidecar, tied them down and sat on the pillion, holding them down. We rolled down the hill towards a crossroads without a chance of stopping. Waiting at the crossroads was my old mate, the bobby, waving us through and we carried on into the football field. As a result of this we could now play proper football on a proper pitch. In the days that followed we would play regularly against other schools and nearby villages. We even took on the RAF boys from Cranwell — serious stuff!

Back to the usual playing around. One game was climbing trees. A fir, which we called a ladder tree because you climbed it like a ladder, was a favourite. Once you made the first branch at the top it was flat so we could lie down in the sun. One day I fell through a soft part and fell from branch to branch before stopping on a fork, the last before the ground. All part of life.

Another day has gone, got to find something to do. We decided we wanted some more arrows for our bows. Our supply was in a field half a mile away where very thin canes — thinner than a pencil grew, and a group of us went looking for the best ones. A man, the foreman of the farm, started to shout and chased us around a nearby field several times. The tallest lad's foot landed in a molehill and the next thing he knew the man's boot kicked him on the backside. The rest of us carried on running, not stopping until we eventually lost him, seven miles past where we lived. After a quick rest we ambled back home in the afternoon, but when we arrived the man was waiting for us so we all split up for home. It was a good thing Roy Watson was a fast runner as he had a lot further to go than the rest of us. He made it home so we all got away. Another lucky escape!

After school each day we would go to the local shop, one of two in the village. With very little money to spend and rationing in full force, a small piece of cheese, some bread and some milk was our only choice (I hated milk _couldn't stand the smell). Luckily, we had a large garden with plenty of hens and a good supply of eggs, not forgetting the local delicacy: the rabbit. They came from poachers or people working on the farms; if you didn't catch them yourself. I must admit I loved the meat, and with plenty of mushrooms it made a fantastic dinner and ensured I had plenty of stamina to keep on running. We were all very active and nobody was fat. That was life then. I don't remember using the local doctor much. Only my grandmother, who was a hypochondriac, would go regularly. I remember walking two miles for the doctor once for her and it turned out there was nothing wrong. That was when we stayed with her on holidays. Then a four-mile walk home with Mum pushing a pram, and back to living with Grandad and Mum's sister. Nothing had changed. The same group of friends.

de Havilland Mosquito

A railway line split the village in two. Our gang stayed together away from school so there was always some rivalry going on. Most of the trouble I got into was with my mates, and plenty more trouble was to follow in the days ahead. Then arrived Wimpey with plenty of lorries to start building an airfield for the Americans. I managed to get a lift on one of their lorries every Saturday. During this time Spitfires, Hurricanes and Mosquitoes were more frequent in the sky. As was the Miles Master, the plane in which we used to train our pilots from Cranwell only two miles away. We were so familiar with these that we knew them by sound alone and we used to test each other on the sound. During the night we often heard night fighters, but they were never seen.

One afternoon I saw a light plane and heard its engine spluttering. I followed it in the sky as it slowly went down towards a woodland. It seemed to miss the trees and I thought it must have made a forced landing. Wrong again! I heard a bang, then saw smoke rising and flames. I jumped on my bike and was one of the first there. I got as near as I could and watched the burning plane. I didn't fancy being the pilot;

another horrible sight. It turned out he had missed the woods and hit the power cables instead. How unlucky can you get?

Days went by and the Yanks started to arrive. My driver took me for a dinner in their canteen. There was a long table with pint mugs on it. Either side were dustbins filled with sugar, white and brown. There was milk, cream, all fruit juices. That was the best dinner I ever had to this day. Soon after, the rest of their cargo started to arrive: Dakotas, Liberators, gliders and, eventually, our paratroopers.

Our village dance hall was a very popular dance to go to, and women would travel up to forty miles to attend. On Saturday night it would be packed with Yanks, RAF locals and Irish (they came over to work in the fields for the farmers). Plenty of fights broke out from all sides, and if they happened to take place under a bedroom window it wasn't unusual for a pot to be emptied over their heads! My cousins used to lay awake on a Saturday night and look out their bedroom windows at our girls and the Americans. I will leave you to guess the rest that happened on many occasions.

Then, one late autumn night, four lads were riding bikes with no lights on — it was a blackout, all curtains were drawn and if the bobby saw any light he would knock on your door and tell you off— when we spotted a beam of light rising in the sky and decided to investigate. We came to a crossroads half a mile from the American base, dropped our bikes and me and another lad climbed a fence, walked a few yards and crept the rest of the way to some bushes, below which we saw a tramp brewing some drink over a fire. He seemed very happy singing away, first in English then in German. We crawled back to our bikes to fetch my mate and tell the bobby what we had seen.

Within seconds he jumped on his bike and shot up the hill in the direction we had just come from. We followed as quickly as we could and arrived just as the American policemen turned up. They arrested him and took him away. I thought he was a German spy. I was pretty sure, in fact. Though we never heard any more about that night, and never will I suppose, that was a very exciting time in my life.

Days later another disaster occurred: an aeroplane crashed a few hundred yards from our home. We were there like a shot to discover that every part of the plane was on fire. I concentrated on the cockpit and again found myself watching someone being burnt. Not a good sight, and something I have never forgotten to this day.

Life was too good to dwell on it though. It was around this time that the sky again began to fill with Dakotas, Liberators and gliders, which often flew astray and made forced landings in the fields nearby. One Saturday, a glider landed in a field close to where we lived. All afternoon they tried to pick it up using two poles and a rope over the top forming a lasso. They failed, and the next morning they towed it further down the field away from the trees, where, all Sunday morning, a Dakota made attempts to pick it up with a hook under the plane's tail. At dinner time it finally succeeded. Up shot the glider! The plane stopped dead in mid-air, the tow rope stretched like elastic then off they flew away. Weekend over.

Back to school Monday, more lessons and playing football on a proper pitch. On the way home one night I was teasing one of the girls, her name was Margaret, when, much to my surprise, she gave me a big kiss. I went on my way, happy as ever, and said goodnight to them all. When I arrived the next morning, hoping to see her again, she was not there. I asked her sister where she was and was told she had died in the night. Another bad day at school.

Time passes — you just don't know what's coming next.

I stood in the school playground looking up in the sky at a squadron of Dakotas right above my head. When I saw two of them clip wings and peel away, they both crashed five miles apart, we were told all crew of both planes died. Another disaster to tell and remember forever.

Christmas has to come the only good meal of the year and cards and presents galore. It was also my birthday that month. That's a laugh. Another year arrived. Farmers worked on their land with the help of German prisoners — they did come in handy. Then, when it was time to gather in the crops, it was the mothers who came in handy picking the spuds, as we called them in Lincolnshire. The farmers sometimes left the women to walk home; that didn't go down well with my mum having to get our meals ready for us four from school. One Sunday morning we went across the road to see what our two cousins were doing. They had a young boy staying there and we were told to take him for a walk. We decided to head for two apple trees, as it was time to pick them, but as usual everything went wrong. The farm, which was managed by one man and many prisoners, was down a narrow lane. Towards his house there was a dip in the ground where two apple trees grew. The trees were full of apples and very easy to climb so, as usual, I volunteered. I was picking and throwing the apples down to the boys when I spotted the farmer as he came charging up the hill, hay fork in hand. I shouted down to my mates and we were already running as fast as we could when, looking back, I saw this young lad laughing at us. Up walked the farmer and stood by him, waiting for us to go back for him. We walked back, wondering what to expect. He just grinned and never said a word. We took the lad and wandered back home, seeing the funny side of it all. Another day in our lives.

Talking about our home — a council house, a wash house with outside toilet joining it. Every Monday morning a fire was lit under a large tub filled with water for the weekly wash. It was a very basic three-bedroom house. There was no central heating, but we had plenty of covers to keep us warm and the kitchen stove was always well stocked up to keep going at night while we sat and listened to the radio for news about the war. Dick Barton was a favourite programme of mine; we also listened to Glenn Miller and Gracie Fields. We had a large garden with a big rhubarb patch and plenty of chickens, meaning we always had an ample supply of eggs and a chicken for Christmas dinner.

That's the life we lived. Winters came and went, going out to the toilet in the cold, shivering, getting back indoors as quickly as I could. At school it was almost as cold inside as out; an old stove gave very little heat unless you sat near it. When spring finally arrived, we could enjoy ourselves as birds and planes again began to fill the sky. Our pilots, in their Spitfires and Hurricanes, seemed to be enjoying life. Little did we know then that we were building up our forces for the retaliation against Hitler. Mustangs started to arrive from America. Now, these planes were a bit special and life was certainly never boring watching them all day long. They made your hair stand on end!

One of the tricks the local boys would get up to — the American airfield was very handy for this — was to wait for the jeeps with their notice to pass by then run across the perimeter to where the planes were standing, climb into their cockpits and pinch fruit and other things which we never had. I was not involved in this and didn't know it was going on.

Then night came with very little to eat, sitting around the fire, talking and listening to the radio about how the war was progressing. Then to a cold bed to sleep.

Monday, a big breakfast then off to school, running all the way, same teacher telling me off for not listening, always in her bad books. I didn't like her one bit so it didn't worry me in the slightest. She lived three doors away so we crossed paths every day.

Soon the sky began to fill up with Lancaster's. Every day they seemed to grow in number, squadron after squadron. It certainly gave us something to look at and admire. Back to earth to talk about the Americans, platoons of them marched through our village almost every day. I used to tag on at the back and heard more than one of them say, 'I don't like him or his mate, the Sergeant. He might get a bullet in his back when overseas. 'They liked handing out chewing gum to the lads and nylon stockings to the women. I didn't like them — so big-headed. I don't think my mates did either. In fact, I am sure.

AVRO Lancaster

One Saturday night I went to fetch a bottle of lemonade from the pub. The landlord went to fetch it and when he came back he said, 'look behind you'. I looked around to see Dakotas dropping our parachutes over their airfield. Or so I thought. It turned out they came down over woods nearby and a few were missing the next morning. We weren't very pleased. They were our men and that didn't help their reputation. Fifty years later I met one of those paratroopers — I will tell you his story later.

One day, when we were playing in the playground at school, we saw a Spitfire chasing a German fighter. They were heading straight for the school when a 'tut, tut' came our way as a teacher came out and told us to go inside and hide under our desks. That lasted a short while until, when we went back outside to play, a lad spotted a hole in the headmaster's chimney pot. Later on, we learnt he had shot the German down near Boston. That's another one less to shoot down.

Winter arrived again, and a run was organised for the whole school, apart from the juniors. It was a long run and the girls had a two-mile head start on the boys. After that, it was catch-up time for us, and I can tell you that a boy won. The rest of the day was like many others at that time: running home from school; open coal fire; very basic meal; huddled together around the fire listening to the radio as our favourite singers lifted our spirits and Churchill lifted our morale; popping outside to the toilet, slippery newspaper for loo paper; then bed, the warmest place in the house.

Next morning it was the same old grind. School was a dead cert now. I was in a class with a male teacher and did start to learn — a bit late but I was trying at least. The seasons moved on to warmer weather and there was more action. Lancaster after Lancaster flew over our houses; it seemed like they never stopped. We guessed where they were going, Germany. We never heard them come home and would listen to the radio at night and wonder how many were missing or shot down.

Men that hadn't been called up to fight went about their working lives. My cousin's dad, the station master, kept the trains moving. Tractors were bringing in loads of sugar beet. This was where the Irish came in, working in the fields and loading trucks for the railway, all towards the war effort. We were always talking about the bombing raids on London. We were lucky in that respect. Grantham suffered two or three raids on the town and a couple of deaths, but we escaped largely unscathed. For a small town not worth bombing we had plenty of air cover fighters at hand to nip up and greet any that tried. We must have been safe.

As the days passed by, we had to entertain ourselves. Our sport depended on the time of the year. Unbeknown to the villagers,

Glenn Miller was entertaining the Americans on their camp. All the top brass was there that night and not a person was sober. Then they flew off Dakota liberators towing gliders and our paratroops heading for the other side of the channel. That night Glenn Miller left for France and has never been seen since.

This part I am telling you comes from an ex-paratrooper I happened to meet about forty-five years back who was there at that time. He told my wife and I he became a prisoner of war after that. I don't think my old mates know about it, if they are still alive now

The tide had turned, and we were advancing across France. The Lancasters were flying overhead every night; their noise never stopped. I wondered how many there were.

Then time for more fun. We happened to wander into a field with lots of cows in it. Little did we know that amongst them was a massive bull who began chasing us. There must have been seven or eight of us and we all ran and dived under some bushes into a ditch where we made our escape. One of the other boys tried to jump over a wire fence and caught one of his legs; it made a right mess of it.

Churchill was on the radio every night and we were all glued to it. The news was good. It was turning out as he predicted, and we were winning at last. Every night I would go to bed excitedly wondering what the next day would bring. Finally, Germany surrendered, and it was time to enjoy ourselves. The radio was full of good news and Churchill was enjoying his prediction: what a man!

Then came the big day and night we set about building a big bonfire; a big pile of tyres as high as you could reach, rubbish as well. When it came time to light it there were no fireworks, so we compromised with other ideas. What a night! Everyone came out to join in the fun, singing and dancing wherever you looked, the sky aglow with fires. That night we went to bed very late.

That's the end of my story.

Good night

War over, School holidays and stayed on a farm belonging to a relative. His name was Elkington, he lived in a village called Mumby, which was seven miles north of Skegness and half a mile from the sea. How I got there I don't remember. Greeting me there was his youngest son Brian and two girls from the north, we were all the same age and got on very well. A relative with a wooden leg and old-fashioned crutches caused by the first world war, another relation with shrapnel in his head caused by that war. We were the farm workers and didn't get paid, we worked for our keep. The girls helped now and again and not forgetting Brian's dad. My first job was digging cattle waste mixed with straw from their winter quarters loading it on a trailer then spreading it on the fields as manure. That was hard work. Getting up at six in the morning, Brian and I would go out in the fields picking mushrooms and filling a large basket with them. Checking the snares for rabbits then taking our find back for a large mushroom and rabbit pie for that dinner. Then the good times: fishing, hanging a line and hook over a bridge, playing football, and running. One of the girls was very tall and a very fast sprinter for a hundred yards, the only person that'd ever beat me. We were forever challenging each other to a race but we never accepted to it. Either way, she knew she would win the hundred yards however I would win the long distance so a stalemate. Then came harvest time Brian's dad would use a scythe to cut the corn twelve feet from the hedge all around the field. Us four, would tie the corn in bundles and stack them out of the way, so the binder was pulled by a tractor driven by the man with the wooden leg, that way we didn't waste any corn. While we were tying up the corn in bundles, the two runners started playing around, wrestling in the stubble. The man with the scythe came back and gave us a black look. After that we went and joined the others. That day over, it was harvest time again, a tractor towed the binder with myself sat on it . In a short while, rabbits started running everywhere, I jumped to the ground to chase a black one, killed it in a ditch and climbed back onto the seat, so the tractor could move on. My face was hit with spray from the tractors radiator. From then on all shotguns were banned. That was a near one for me. Locals used to come and shoot and capture the rabbits in all the fields we harvested, so it was a busy time for all of us. The next job was to bring in the corn for the winter, that meant loading on a hay rack-I was standing in it with Brian with a hay fork in my hand while the rest of the people forked up the corn to us. We had to pack it around us and piled them higher making sure we would not fall off it. Then we sat down there whilst a horse towed the cart back to the farm over the rough terrain hoping not to fall off. Another test in life. Then we needed some free time. Playing with the girls at night, Brian and I would go outside with a torch and hay fork trying to bring down the bats that were flying in the air. I got lucky one night and knocked one down, picked it up took it indoors and plonked it on my tormentor's hand. The girl I mentioned earlier chased me all around the farmyard in the dark-She never forgot about me putting a bat in her hand. My farming holiday then came to an end and we went back home.

With my bike at Ancaster Fair

At school in Ancaster I was growing vegetables on the school allotment. I finished building up a dry-stone wall, no-one wanted to do it apart from me. I remember the headmaster coming to look at it, I think he suggested to my dad that building was for me as I was about to start work. I started on an apprenticeship scheme as an apprentice bricklayer. We had a qualified bricklayer and joiner. They taught the lads their trades. The bricklayers did everything, digging trenches and concreting them for the brick footings which we did-The joiners did the labouring, we dug the trenches for the drains which were deep. While I was digging away one caved in on me so that I was trapped waist high, my companions had to dig me out. In my years of training we built a row of houses from top to bottom, including the roof tiles. The joinery work was done by the apprentice joiners. We went to night school for the drawing aspect of our work: learning all the bonds, setting out and putting levels and a good all-rounding for the building industry. During the dinner hour I was wrestling with some of the other lads on site another favourite pastime was me and my friends swimming in a river nearby where were staying.

Grantham Town Hall

My next story is how I got to work and back home. Distance was just over eight miles both ways, that meant riding a pushbike, sit up and beg. Fortunately, I had company, two chaps quite a bit older had racing bikes. That meant trying to keep up with them. Russell Bentley was one and the other was Roy Watson's brother. Most days it was a good ride others were the opposite-One morning, frost was hanging on the trees and cables .As we set off for work from our village we had this steep hill to climb-The road was covered in sheet ice trying to climb this was impossible. The back wheel had just spun you would fall off, you would just have to walk the rest. But we managed to get to work somehow-We always got there, no matter how bad the conditions-Most days it would be a race. Another morning it was raining very heavily and a strong head wind. We used capes which were long to keep you dry. Climbing that steep hill was impossible I had to walk; with so much wind resistance it took a very long time to get to work about three times longer. Going home that night if I remember it took twenty minutes. One morning up the same hill ,at the top was this airfield the Americans used during the last war-Glen Miller was there, RAF Cranwell used it to train our pilots because it has concrete runways. Cranwell did not have them, we saw at least six planes that had crashed all nose down and tail up we heard that it was their solo night flight. One crashed and the rest followed.

I left the apprenticeship scheme got posted to a building firm called Fosters the largest in Grantham. One winter, I had a job undercover we were working late until seven in the evening. That morning it rained heavily it slowly turned to snow(four to six inches deep)then it started to freeze that night .In the dark riding home the roads were very dangerous ruts with ice and frozen snow, if you had one wheel in a rut and one in another you would fall. I once came to a junction to turn left the bike went horizontal the pedal caught the rut I stood upright on my feet. Further on going down a small incline I came off in front of a bus I managed to get my bike away from the bus, I had a lot further to get home. I forgot to tell you what happened when I got home ate my dinner each night in the spring or autumn I would play football after tea. When I was old enough for the pub my next place in the dark nights was drinking very little. The dart board was inviting to me I became quite good at it, then in a short period I got picked for the pub team. That meant playing against other pubs in the area, mostly on a Friday night. We used to travel there by taxi, two or three cars hired from the only garage in the village. We used our own drivers to take us to the matches. One Friday we had a match on about nine miles away-Our driver was a local chap just out of the army, we all had a good game won the match and celebrated with having a drink and a chat-Time to go home, outside it was very thick with fog like the one I experienced in London. We set off for home, I sat at the back between two long distance lorry drivers in the leading car. All of a sudden, these two chaps bellowed out. Our driver instantly stopped. These two chaps dragged him out and off his seat. One took over and I managed to see out of the window that there were land mines surrounding us. We were on an airfield perimeter in a very dangerous place. We did get home safely though and not a word was said.

Saturday morning came work after breakfast and I got my bike out, then I got called up for the RAF square bashing for eight weeks. Two weeks and we caught a train to Bridgnorth. It was raining all day the day we arrived. We were given a barrack to stay in, I made for a stove and a bed next to it. Then we had to go around the camp to collect our bedding and other things-Now it was snowing very heavily our bedding got damp-Next morning, it had frozen six inches of snow and ice that meant trying to march on the snow for the first time. All day long, we were shouted at to dig our heels in. Day over, back at the billet I lit the fire in the stove while the other lads were getting their ablutions done, polishing their boots so that you could see your face in them. That helped on parade next morning it would go down in their good books and give you a good name. Then I would do my washing and shaving in cold water. When I came back to enjoy the fire, everyone was sat round it, even on my bed. Morning came the same old thing. Marching in the freezing cold the water towers in all the squares were solid ice. The recruits were given jobs like cleaning the sinks and toilets with cold water which were impossible to clean to RAF standards people were put on a charge.

Every morning the camp doctor would visit each hut. One person was very ill in the first week he was carried off to a hospital we never saw him again. Two weeks later, I was not very good either-I was hoping to see the doctor, he never turned up. Another lad in the same hut had the same problem as me. He decided to go on special sickness' decided to go on parade. As usual it was freezing but a lovely sunny morning. Six o'clock in the morning within ten minutes we were told to stand to attention-I passed out and fell flat on my face. They picked me up and carried me to my billet. There was this other chap they had turned him away. Then things did start to happen...Back we went to the camp hospital, we were met by an orderly corporal he asked what we were doing. he told us to go back in a nasty way. My friend stood his ground and looked him straight in the face. He disappeared and came back with a thermometer. He took our temperatures. He went white and quiet they were very high. Next thing we knew we were in bed.

I could not remember the next few days. My friend was rushed to a hospital in Birmingham-I never saw him again. Two weeks later I came out. They gradually worked me back to square bashing. Snow had not melted all night. Dig your heels in all day. Then rumours were going around the hut about a dark skinned lad as the saying goes he was trying to work his ticket. Apparently, our corporal would beat him up because he was so obnoxious. He was in the group before us. While we were there, he was in the guardhouse which he did not like. He used the guard's boot as a toilet that was the rumour going around. Then one frosty morning our corporal was drilling us on the square. Then out of the corner of my eye, I spotted this chap being escorted off the camp. Our corporal saw him. He made our squad turn around to put us between the chap and him. Two sergeants were dragging him off the camp. I did not know what would happen if he reached our corporal. That day he was discharged. Now square bashing was over, we got posted to our next camp to train for airfield construction for one month. Next posting was to get kitted out to Cyprus for that ongoing war. Walking round this camp having my first X-Ray. Later on I got called back for another X-Ray. A girl and a chap both of their X-rays eliminated the girl. That left us to two men. They said go and get a weekend pass and on Monday report for more X-rays. Eventually they did more of them. Then we were in the camp hospital. That night the nurses would have put our food under the door if they could. Next morning an ambulance took us to a hospital near

Swindon. I cannot remember the name it seemed a very efficient place. Any type of drink we wanted ,juices of any kind and beer on your locker. Every day, I did see some horrible sights of humans with scars and bruises all over their bodies. Eventuality I was discharged, how long I was there I do not remember.

Now it was catch-up time. I did not go abroad. I eventually turned up on a camp near Stratford-upon-Avon. It was called Wellesbourne Mountford. My one and only job was in the barrack store. A good part of it was going around the county taking inventory of RAF staff living quarters, bedding and crockery and reporting back to camp driven in a lorry by a civilian. This camp gave me a chance to play darts in the mid-morning, dinner and evening. Before long, I was winning all the games .1 entered camp knockout and got in the final three times but never played it. I then decided to confront the corporal that was running them, it turned out he was pocketing the money. He said go to the camp dance which was every second Wednesday so I did. I won every spot waltz and other prizes for about a month. One minute I decided to walk to a village pub to organise a darts match against the pub. Not properly dressed, I wore the wrong hat when I came out of the pub the camp police were waiting for me and put me on a charge for not wearing the correct hat.

Next day, I went in front of the commanding officer. Two military policemen escorted me in and the commanding officer asked me what I was doing. I told him I was organising a darts match and I mentioned the hat which did not suit me. He just smiled and discharged me I noticed long faces from the coppers.

As I left the camp it gave me a chance to hitch hike home at weekends. I had mishaps, one going on the Al going north. I got a lift in a posh car. One April we were heading for Grantham, at the top of the hill into Grantham there was a tractor and a trailer parked on our side. Coming up the other way was a car and caravan. My driver braked hard on the wet road and slithered from side to side down the hill. Bouncing off the trailer and tractor on my side, he clipped the caravan by his side. We never stopped and carried on into town and called at the police station I got out and thanked him and then he drove home to the company he owned. I went home the next weekend my mother showed me the local paper mentioning that the driver had been fined.

Our wedding

I will tell you about another incident. Going home one Friday night in the winter I got a lift in an articulated lorry. Travelling from Leicester to Melton Mowbray it was snowing very heavy. Going down a steep hill the back started to overtake the front. Luckily he was a good driver it righted so I got home alright. That meant I could play darts at the pub with my mates. my darts paid for my weekend at home it was very rare if I lost. Going back to camp was not that easy sometimes I had to walk the last nine miles but it was worth it. Then I got a posting from Wellesbourne Mountford to Newquay at St. Everall two miles away. I was there for a month it was spring time then I got discharged from the RAF-Back in Civvy Street and work at my old firm. My parents had moved to Grantham from Ancaster that meant getting to know other people .I joined with my brother and his mates going to other pubs and dances in the town darts was played occasionally. One night my brother took me to see one of his friends. A girl sat on a lads knee. The next time we went there she came on and sat on my knee I was very surprised-From then on we courted for a year or two she told me her parents were moving down to Bracknell. I asked her if she was going down with them she said no. I was not the only pulling power she was a member of the town swimming club and town champion diver, as well as doing judo-One Sunday night I was asked to come to her house her dad sat opposite to me and said Shirley has changed her mind he said to me are you coming I said no I have done enough travelling he replied you're scared. There is only one answer to that I will come . So Bracknell here we come and I moved into their new house.

Her dad had a job planned and Shirley started off as a secretary which was her job so I had to find one. Luckily a school was being built close by Polish chaps. I got a job at once-Her mum stayed at home. Working with these Polish people turned out to be a very good thing. I got on well as people they were very good workers and good at their job. I learnt a few Polish tricks of the trade. Later on they came handy in working life. Ted was the boss he told us about the last war he was a prisoner of that war. I can't remember whether it was the Germans or the Russians it could have been both. we built that school and moved on to other buildings. That meant getting the bike out and travelling long distances eventually a scooter to a school further away. That was a bit too far. Then when I needed a pastime, Sperry's had a dance hall which Shirley and I went to on a Saturday night. Then we joined a scooter club that meant other things to do. We went on trips at weekends down to the coast in a group-I was Tail-end Charlie had a job keeping up with them although my scooter was the fastest. Luckily I always managed to do it.

A year later we moved to a village a mile away which did not stop us from doing the same things. It was a quiet place apart from two breakouts at Broadmoor hospital, which was very scary. The Army and police were searching our sheds and gardens-We all lost a lot of sleep until they caught them. The next big thing to happen was a wedding. Ours was a honeymoon on the Isle of Wight-We enjoyed it and had good weather .My next thing was finding somewhere to live. We found a bungalow in a place called Woodley we agreed the terms and bought it with a small mortgage as I had enough money to put down for the rest. Two bedrooms,a big garden which was just the job for the two of us. Then I decided to find work nearby as well as new friends. Scooter club was out of the question. Then we sorted our bungalow out. As time passed by I decided to work for myself and employ others. I was getting plenty of money and I expanded and grew more money coming in. Then I used to wake up early in the morning planning the day ahead. That was part of the job and life you don't get money for nothing. So I thought we needed something to do at weekends. We bought a tent and went camping with Shirley's mum and dad in Spain, her dad used his car for at least two summers. Then I used my first car to Spain another year. Later on I decided to buy a small sailing dinghy. In 1966 we were on holiday in Saundersfoot Wales, on the beach when England won the World Cup everyone had radios on it was fantastic, we could have been there. Sailing out to sea, got talking to a man then met his wife from High Wycombe. Have been friends ever since we met. We met up once every two weeks. When my wife was alive, we had dinner parties and sailed in the past tense-We still meet up only three of us now my wife has gone. Going back to sailing I joined a club near Bognor and bought a static caravan nearby I sailed every weekend from Easter to October. Eventually, I became quite good at it. After racing against national champions every week, I became club champion for a few years.

One story I must tell you about was in the winter I went shopping with my wife on a Saturdays, on the way home a car ran into the back of my car. He paid for the damage. About two years later, out sailing with my crew off Littlehampton about a mile offshore I spotted something flashing from further out .We decided to investigate, we eventually found the cause. It was a small fishing boat with father and son on it he was about nine miles out with no life jackets on. The engine had broken down with no spare. I looked at him and realised it was the same person that ran into my car two years back-We towed him back to our club and left him there but he never said thank you.

We sailed for about thirty years, Shirley came every weekend. Then our daughter was born. After a short while she came too and had plenty of friends to play with on the beach. Until one autumn sailing over going to work one day I got held up in a traffic jam and spotted a run-down house for sale I liked the look of it and I had to put a bid to the council. Three months later, it was accepted cash up front. In this short time there was a slump in the housing market. That meant I had a job selling the old one. It took about three months to sell it. The money became a problem, by now I had some large contracts. I had to borrow a small amount of money to buy it. I did manage to keep going eventually until a woman bought it. She came to see my wife in the daytime when I was at work. Then I set to work using the boys to repair the house. That was a lot of time and money spent. We cut out an old wall and made two rooms into one. A small lounge added a small extension new kitchen and bathroom, in time we got the job done. Over the years I trained quite a few of my lads who were willing workers (two of them were brothers). Thy are now very wealthy as I got them their first contract. Wherever I worked, I was given apprentices to look after and train.

Now I had to find a sport that I could learn it was golf. I played every Sunday. That day I did not stop my work and my daughter joined me, we improved very quickly-She joined a good club as a junior member that helped me to get into that same club. and at weekends, Shirley and I would see Pat and Eric. Every two weeks we would have a meal out and a walk. That's when I started to play golf. Eric suggested a game as we were walking around a public golf course. Then I said lets try this game. We both did that day. I carried on he did not. Then came more good times they bought a yacht so we had the chance to go with them, it was moored at Portsmouth. We sailed over to the Isle of Wight quite a few times. We were coming back from there and sailed past a boat with Prince Charles in it-Down below they were diving for the remains of the Mary Rose we always had something to talk about and do. One night they asked us if we wanted to go sailing next weekend. They said be down at Haven Island at the Saturday morning Shirley and I were well on time and found their boat and them as usual. Pat was always talking to someone. I kept saying to myself lets go eventually we left. The tide was going out very fast within twenty minutes we were touching the mud we were aground. We backed the main sail put the engine on and wriggled free. Off we went again, not long before the same trouble, same method to free us. By now boats were stranded all around us. We never gave up four or five times it happened, till eventually we were in open water. Ahead was a gap out to open sea that was Chichester bar, that vast area was called Chichester Harbour, we sailed through. I said to Eric pull the main sail up as it had been up and down a few times.

He started pulling the sail up. The halyard went up the mast but no sail. The shackle had come undone the next problem was getting it down to fix the main sail on. I suggested making a harness out of towels to put around myself we then tied the spinnaker halyard to me. I then started to climb the mast, Shirley, Pat and Eric were pulling on the halyard at the same time, eventually I made it to the spreaders ,it's a tee section three quarters up the mast. I got there one foot either side of the mast, the next problem reaching the top .I suggested pass the spinnaker pole up to me, that had a hook on both ends and a line between the two hooks, the next problem reaching up to the top with the boat swaying a good yard .I kept on trying and trying, I had to have a rest. I looked down below I saw a creature swimming round the boat about two feet from the hull it was about eight feet long. I shouted down there's a shark joking it was a dolphin. I think it was there to save me they are well known for protecting humans from sharks out to sea eventually I managed to get the hook fixed to the shackle passed the pole down the mast then up went the sail then out to sea we would go for the day it was fantastic. Then we set for home. That's all worth talking about.

Occasionally, we had barbecues with friends, trips on the river with Pat and Eric, meals in a pub and not forgetting gardening. I have forgotten to mention my daughter who had settled down with two granddaughters (two smashers)! Out of the blue, we decided to downsize our house, so we put it on the market. It then got sold and we moved to an apartment. This was all done in four weeks so we were nearer to our daughter and family nearby. Then we had to start a different way of life, living close to neighbours took a lot of getting used to. Less work, no gardening, all we had was one bedroom and a kitchen. We got to know new people and visit lots of nearby shops.' have forgotten holidays, the last one for the two of us.

HOLIDAYS

The Holidays I have had in the past are worth telling, some fantastic memories. I will start with the early ones. Spain, the first, we went camping just after getting married, drove there by car. Shirley's mum and dad came too. We camped by the sea at a place called Calla Go, a nice spot for swimming, a big camp site with plenty to do, nearby was a small town which had a small bullring. We saw quite a few bull fights. The last one, they couldn't kill the bull, the matadors and toreadors and picadors couldn't ; they enticed a cow in likewise it enticed the bull out and I have never known that to happen, and I have seen a few. The crowd were not very pleased with a lot of booing-We did go back to the same place other years as we liked it and places nearby.

Our next trip was Italy, our first stop was Lake Como. We put the tents up and wandered around admiring the scenery, the mountains, until the clouds came over; it looked like a lot of rain so we decided to move on to Venice,it turned out to be a very good idea. The weather was fantastic, we stayed on the beach all day, at night we left the lido by boat to Venice every night to see the attractions: Bridge of Sighs, Doges Palace, and all the canals and lots of things to see and do. It was a very good holiday, three weeks we had there, then we drove back home, then caught the ferry back.

Our next trip was to Yugoslavia camping. In my car I overtook a Merc going up a 1 in 5 hill loaded with camping gear in a small Vauxhall.

We had a short break from long holidays overseas as I was very busy with work that had priority. In fact it was a long break caused by work, that meant money but made up for it by going down to Swanage every year it turned out forty all told, never missed a year. We loved the place I still do. Going back this year 2020.

Then it was time to start travelling to far off places. My first was Canada we landed at

Calgary, there we picked up a camper van, had a few lessons, then out to the Rockies to Banff saw Banff Spring Hotel hot springs and wandered around, fantastic. Next day we drove to Lake Louise had a look at the chateaus, the lake and the background with a glacier in the distance. Another day there the next day we drove past Snake Pass wherever you looked fabulous, then on to Athabasca ice fields, plenty of people about admiring the ice, they were walking on the glacier. The glacier was so rough to tread on, dangerous too, they had trips in a bus with very wide tyres up the glacier. Time passed by, it was getting dark. We decided to stay the night on a camp site. we parked on our spot a concrete slab with plenty of logs at hand and a barbecue . In the roof of the van was an axe you could shave with it. I then chopped the wood up for lighting it took a long time to get going, then I put two gigantic steaks on the fire with jacket potatoes. It took a long time to cook and eat but it was a very lonely place one other van there a bit scary high on the top of the mountains. Then, next day we saw Athabasca Falls and Johnston Canyon.

Our next port of call was Jasper, we went up to the top by tramway. Then on to Maligne Lake, it's only twenty miles from Jasper. It was discovered by an Englishman years ago after seeing other places, mountains either side. It's great there are plenty of lakes all over Emerald Lake was fantastic.

On the way to Vancouver Island, I decide to go another route via Whistler right over the highest mountains in the Rockies, a sign saying it was. We stopped for a rest. Along came two motorbikes with big chaps on them. it was a bit scary as Shirley and I were alone. We spoke they turned out, they were very friendly. We then decided to to go down this hill for Whistler. In a short while the road turned to gravel. We went round this S bend, I then decided to go back, there was a bear waiting for us. I stopped, got my camera, it then ran away. We then had a long run to the main road for Vancouver, a good two days wasted. We arrived at Vancouver, caught a ferry to the Island, we saw Victoria, then French Beach near by, old wooden boats, then paid a visit to the end of a road on the west side, then caught a ferry to the mainland, then started to head back to Calgary by another route. We stopped off at a camp site. That night I went to the toilets, started to talk to a stranger he said he had just been to that island, he had made arrangement to meet a friend there the idea was to walk that part of the west coast, his friend didn't go, so he went on his own, he said it was fantastic all the wild life sharks, whales. He pitched his tent on the beach one night, next morning found bear footprints round his tent. Next morning set off for Calgary.

I decided to have a rest from driving, pulled into a lay-by, parked near buses, then decided to walk up this mountain amongst trees. Shortly we heard voices coming down we met and started talking, four ladies. I asked one where she came from she said Nottingham, a nurse there. Two minutes later I ask again the same answer of the third time she admitted a small hamlet half a mile from Ancaster my village, she went to my school. Back to Calgary and back home, a great holiday.

Next year another one this time Australia by van. We flew to Brisbane, travelled all the way up Queensland coast, stopping at all the towns to Cairns . A very interesting and tiring journey driving a two way road very narrow road rolled of into sand either side: windows down music on singing away, Shirley asleep, coming towards us a very large lorry half on my side of the road. I just managed to stay on the road coming up behind another lorry. I was very worried at this point he stayed on his half, the first driver must have fallen asleep. We called at most places on the way up Dunk Island was one of the main stopping points, we left the van ashore while we caught a ferry over 10 minutes to get there. A lovely spot wandering around with a small airfield there, palm trees sandy beaches and plenty to do then went back at night ,back over next morning we did that four or five days then travelled further on through the tea plantations over narrow gauge train lines till we arrived at Cairns. Plenty to do, we were taken to the Barrier Reef , we went snorkelling, swimming from a boat, then saw the crew throw food out the back to feed the fish, many of all kinds. We took a trip on a yellow submarine, a good time we had, then on the way back at Whit Sundays we did the usual out at sea by boat saw some sharks, and some weird creatures on the beach and in the bushes, then we drove back to Cairns then flew home.

Next year came along where shall we go: New Zealand and Rarotonga and Aitutahu. We flew to Rarotonga stayed in a small hotel complex lovely spot, ate out every day it was a small island hot and sunny with a road all around it fifty yards from the sea. A bus went both ways, you could get off where you liked and get on. Tropical trees and bushes one end a place called Muri beach and a sailing club and food sold there, a fantastic place to relax and have a good holiday. At the end we flew by small plane for twenty minutes to the island Aitutaki, landed, taken to our bungalow for two. It had a thatched roof, a tropical garden,all round verandahs, (numbers two) over the sea inlet, divers, swimmers, every thing you wanted to do, boats out fishing, Paradise, flowers on your pillow every night. Your hotel was fantastic, you're living a dream, wish it would never end. It did we then flew to Christchurch New Zealand-There we picked up another camper van, got the hang of it then our journey began.

We headed right through the centre of the South Island towards Greymouth through a mountain range finished up having a puncture, pumped the tyre up but managed to get to Greymouth had it repaired, had a look around went in a museum, then decided to head north. A sort of ring road round the Island, stopped off to look at the scenery, called at some villages now and again our favourite shops were their antiques old English bits and pieces, plates cups back to our forties, we stopped to have a rest. A bridge to our right with a big lake looked interesting, so we walked over. We didn't get to the other side we were bitten by some mites we couldn't stand the bites so we ran back to the van and moved on to Picton, the gateway by ferry to the North Island, an interesting place to look at,then carried on down to Arrow Town an early gold mining settlement, the usual shops. Further down the coastal road we stopped, there was a helicopter flight out to over the sea, whale watching, informing the boats below where they were. Another fantastic flight for Shirley and myself. Time to move on down south, we turned right to go to Greymouth, we arrived then went south and inland to Queenstown. we did stay here for awhile, we had a ride on TSS EARLSLAW on Lake Wakatipu heading for the colonels homestead where they kept sheep. A good day out, we had a good look around, we then found they did a trip by coach down to Milford Sound, it was a day trip. When we got there it was wet, plenty of rain. we learnt later on we could have flown that way the weather would have been known, we could have chosen a better day. Next day we set off to see Mount Cook we arrived at the foot, fantastic sight, we wandered around talking to people. One told us they do flights over it. In the meantime we had a ride up the glacier by an Australian in his four-by-four. After we were told that there was an airfield twenty miles away, a camp site nearby, we called at the airfield ,a pilot told us that if we gave him a phone number he would ring and let us know if the weather was right. We did get a call so off we went, found his plane. Up we went over the top of the mountain: we could see the glacier and others too. We could see the coasts on either side of the island, the camera came out I haven't seen that before-We could see mount Tasman and Franz Josef, Fox Glaciers and the Tasman Sea. Then we saw the Hackett bridge near Arrowtown ,bungee jumping over Shotover River, and bridge leading to Hanmer Springs bungee jumping and jet boating. Holidays over we flew back home. We had some very good memories after that trip.

Then came a long break from my trips a broken back in four places and right foot and leg that took about four years to make a comeback. I eventually asked them to take my right leg off. At the third time of asking they took it off, then more work adapting to my situation. I did win, got back to golf, then more holidays to come, I decided Argentina. The trip was to Buenos Aires: we stayed there four days wandered around admiring the colourful houses, there was an area of them all, then we saw them horse riding and jumping cowboys as known, it was well worth watching. We then flew over the Andes mountains to Chile. We landed near the coast, can't remember that place, boarded a ship that night , within half an hour the wind got up horrendous, nearly every person on board was seasick including my wife. I decided to go to the restaurant for dinner, there were about three people there. I found a table for two in an alcove, then along came a man put his head round the corner and said can I join you. Yes, I said, only us turned up. We had our meal and sat chatting for a while, that was the beginning of a great friendship. The boat travelled all the way down the coast stopping off at places one was size like a hangar selling goods in a market under cover. we were told not to take any money out, keep it in a concealed place on you. The boat stopped off ,we got off to have a look. When we got back on four or five people had been robbed. We then moved on down the coast stopping and looking at glaciers and other places of interest. We called in at Ushire, it's a port where they ship people and goods out there to Antarctica. Later on another holiday, I met an Australian,t hey shipped tents toilets and other equipment for a fantastic holiday, (Antarctica) we carried on until we rounded a corner past the Horn the sea was like a millpond ,flat as a pancake. All of us drank wine and smoked a cigar, then we started heading inland up the Magellan Straits ,in a short while the wind picked up. It was so strong a pilot boat was coming out to meet us. We were docking at this place Punta Arenas; That strait was one of the windiest places on the planet. They put ropes across the roads so people could walk across, anyway that boat had to turn around and to go back, we carried straight on ,heading back in the same direction via another route. we were out at sea such a long time I organised a whist drive, that helped to pass the time away. We eventually docked, then flew home. Tom and Marge are still my friends since then, all my holidays included then Swanage this March.

I think my next holiday was to the Seychelles. As a starter, we arrived, stayed in a hotel for two days, enjoying the sunshine, swimming as usual, then we boarded a tall Russian sailing ship bunks below, no air conditioning and it was very hot. We set off under sail as the wind was blowing, when it dropped the engines came on. We travelled at night , next morning we were anchored about half a mile from an island. After breakfast we got ready for a day out, camera, swim gear. We climbed down a ladder on the side of this big boat into a

Zodiac,then headed towards this island. We stopped half way, slipped over the side for a swim or a snorkel or diving,then we went to the beach,pulled onto dry sand,then we went to investigate right round the island. At the end amongst palm trees there was a small graveyard, another part, old shacks made of corrugated sheets, wrought iron beds, not a soul on the island. We spent the whole day there,then went back to the boat each Zodiac had a doctor. Meal times apart from breakfast the doctors served our meals, very good food made by Russians.

There were Ukrainian staff on board,about twenty Ukrainian men on board of age twenty,they cleaned the ship, sorted the ropes and general dogsbodies and took it in turn, taught them to navigate by the stars,nice bunch of men. Our holiday was a month all told so that ship travelled by night,sail or motor depending on the wind,so next morning we were anchored off another island. Every day the same thing, breakfast, Zodiac over the side, a swim or dive, then on this new island to explore. This happened for about 9 islands, could be more, I never counted. Every one was enjoying their holiday every day, life was a dream. We were anchored off another two islands to investigate then a vast lagoon nearby. We were about twenty miles off the African coast this trip, the Australian took us in his Zodiac to see the lagoon. the water was so clear and tidal you could see the sharks, stingrays, every type of fish, the lagoon was very large, then the Aussie said it is tidal we will have to go back. The next minute the propeller was grinding on the coral, he turned the engine off jumped in the water and pushed us to deeper water. So back to the main boat on board you had a lot to see and do; you could climb the rigging to the crow's nest, many did including that German doctor I have a photo of her climbing on to the bridge to watch what was happening. The

Australian took Shirley and I down below to show by film the holiday in Antarctica.

The day before the end of our fantastic holiday the Australian said be on deck about 7 that night. We all turned up on time he stood behind a barbecue, with an apron on next to four other cooks he said help yourself: crab, lobster of a very large size, other type of fish, steaks, the largest I have seen, drinks of all kind all free. After we all had finished we all sat out on the deck in groups playing instruments with all singing, not many sober, all looking up at the stars. A night I shall never forget. That was a holiday organised by two Australian brothers judging by what we had and what was on offer ,no other holidays half as good. Brilliant.

Another year has gone. Time to take another trip abroad this time to Malaysia. We settled in at a hotel would have been for two nights, the hotel was called Ferringhi Beach Hotel about 4 miles from Penang. We were waiting for a car to take around this country we had to wait about four days late it was booked for quite a few days. We were told it had to be back at a certain time. We put our cases in the boot and set off by-passing Penang, taking my time getting used to it and the roads. I was driving to a place called (Hipyo) during the last war our soldiers were stationed there. When we arrived in the town looking for our hotel it started to rain. I had never seen it like this before. we stopped by a parade ground our troops used to use within minutes it was a great lake all cars had to stop ,that was my first experience of a monsoon. Two days later we set off for the Cameron Highlands had a long climb. At the top was a tea plantation we saw them picking the leaves then went back to a small village where we found a place to stay, very scruffy ,not much choice, only a night. We then set off back down to the bottom of the hill , a bit scary, sharp bends, narrow road a steep drop on one side. Our next place we headed for a small town and a harbour. We stayed in a hotel for about a week. Every morning we would catch a ferry across to the island Pulau Pangkor. we would stay there the whole day exploring, very interesting. They did accommodation Pan Pacific Resort. This Island was very popular the ferries were always full, really full. We decided to head back to Penang and our hotel as the cars had to be back at such a time with a full tank. on the way we stopped off at a small town as I saw a sign of a travel agent. I went inside she was an English woman from Brighton, her husband owned the shop. We were in luck he booked us on a flight from Penang to Phuket, Thailand we paid him for the tickets, we wouldn't get them till we got to Penang Airport was a bit worried so we set off back to our hotel to take the car back. It was a long journey. we went round the outskirts of Penang looking for a petrol station, not one. Time was getting on, we went past our hotel to the next village no petrol. as we went by the hotel I saw this car come rushing out and it stayed close to us, anyway we turned round and went back to the hotel as no petrol, car still behind. We pulled in there was this woman waiting for us we were with five minutes to spare, hand it over had to pay for the petrol. We stayed in the hotel that night. Next morning we set off for the airport our tickets were waiting for us. Off we went to Phuket not a long flight. We landed, a car took us to our new hotel, a posh one with a swimming pool and the lot, a very good room. It was getting late before we settled into our room, so we decided to go for a walk along the sea front. It was so hot. A stall was selling drink with ice in. We didn't know ice was in till we realised , then stopped but it was too late. We had a short walk,being as it was a new place, went back to our room in a short while both started to rush to the toilet. We were fighting each each other to get in, all night long it lasted, and next day I found a doctor nearby. He gave us something that helped. we couldn't leave the hotel for four days, lucky we had a swimming pool on hand.

After that episode we did start exploring one was coral Island snorkelling and the usual,then we visited another island and (Phargraves Bay) towards James Bond Island which was very interesting. We did see some elephant training, interesting how calm they were. Then we set off through the mangrove to Phang Nga Bay towards Bond Island. On the way to these islands we passed a town on stilts a Muslim fishing village that's what it was. It had a school and a football pitch and a mosque. We stopped by a jetty on stilts walked on rough planks toward a place to eat, I looked at the food that's all I don't like spicy stuff to put it bluntly I couldn't eat. (the first time was at the airport to fly home about two weeks). It was interesting looking at this strange place on stilts bits of wood floating in the water below toilets waste ended in the water not a nice place to live. The island of the Bond film was very interesting we spent a long time looking around. I think that's all I have to say about this holiday.

Next trip South Africa, we stayed in a hotel in Zimbabwe had a tour around the place. I then booked a breakfast trip on the Zambezi river. We got there early expecting to see a few people about and Shirley and I asked what was going on a man said it's only you two. We got in this smallish boat the helmsman and the cook we weren't very far from the Victoria Falls, we kept going nearer crocodiles all around and the odd hippo then the cook started on our breakfast egg, bacon, the lot. I told the cook to join us. The four of us sat eating having a good chat then I looked down we weren't far from the falls. That was the best meal I have had the sky was brilliant we were very happy. Shirley and I , we then went to Cape Town, we stayed just on the outskirts , next day we caught transport to the waterfront as usual wandered around, we heard that a murder had just taken place we were told that was common. Then we caught a boat to Robben Island had an interesting trip hearing about the prison and internees. A day later on we boarded a steam train which travelled the garden route; it took about a week, very interesting , stopping at a lot of places en route, we had to keep the door locked and the window shut. On the way back to Cape Town the train stopped at a level crossing we had to get off with our cases and walked over there was our transport to take us back. I was very worried it was so dark we couldn't see a thing. It was waiting for us. we drove back to Cape Town so that we could catch our flight to Mauritius to stay at Colonial Coconut Hotel right on the sea front. Our daughter joined us on this Island on the water's edge was a small boat that would take you out snorkelling. The daughter had a few trips then I hired a car and driver to take us right round the Island, he was a Tamil. We called in at Port Louis had a look round a Tamil temple was very interesting. Tamil ladies dressed in lovely clothes and headgear and the buildings then past a golf course saw a tea plantation, Indian film crew. When we got back to our hotel had a trip on a tall ship then another trip on a catamaran. I think that's all I can remember about this holiday so back we flew home.

Sri Lanka

We flew to Colombo, a very busy town, the traffic was terrible. when we came out of the airport we met our driver, he asked where we wanted to go, we had two weeks in his car, we will go up to Kandy. we set off to strange places, we stopped and got out of his car, had a look round, every night we stopped at a hotel, he stayed in the annexe. The next day we would go to another destination, same thing, exploring on route. We stopped at Kandy, then headed for our destination. The exciting part: in a short while we stopped at a ruined city that had been lost in the jungle for a few hundred years. It had a large population all those years back. It was so big you needed some form of transport. It was very interesting, old ruins of all sorts, all day we were there, then we set off. All of a sudden an elephant came out of the jungle , stood in the road . Our driver stopped his car, said don't make a noise. other cars stopped behind, ten minutes later on it moved into the jungle on the other side. The next day we came across a fortress ruins on a rock of Sigiriya. The story we were told a tribe was surrounded for a long time by his brother's tribe, you could climb it if you wanted. We were then moved on to Nuwara Eliya the tea plantations , saw them pick tea. our next call was elephant orphanage, saw their keepers washing them, then we went to another hidden city called Anuradhapura. Polonnaruwa Dagoba Temple built with millions of bricks nearly 1,000 years ago, the ruins of Anuradhapura capital in 380 BC.

There was a hell of a lot including Buddha. we eventually stopped at our hotel for the next two weeks, it was right on the beach, ideal for swimming. One day I came across a wedding amongst the trees, it looked a gorgeous event, elephant all dressed up, the locals in their gowns. The couple were English, that's how to get married. At the back of our hotel nearby was the train from Colombo to Galle. Right at the back of the line a road covered the same route. One day I hired a car and driver to take us to Galle. On the way we saw stilt fishermen. We then stopped off at a very small mine. A man went down this hole with a bucket , fetched stones which were turned into jewels in a small shed nearby. They made a ring with a jewel in it. I bought one for Shirley, paid for it, they brought it to the hotel the next night. We then went on to Galle. It was a very interesting place. we visited the fort; it had a wall keeping the sea out. There was a nice walk around the top, it had a Magistrates court below a lighthouse. There was A Dutch church and a temple all built by the Dutch. It was run down in places. We had a meal at a nice bay in the shade from the sun, we then went back to our hotel. Next night Shirley's ring arrived had more days there then flew home another holiday over.

Iceland

The start of a wonderful holiday we arrived and moved into a hotel at Reykjavik, went sightseeing saw fantastic falls then went skidooing had a good time. We then flew to Husavik wandered around then went whale watching at midnight in the daylight, then flew back to Husavik. In our hotel, we were told to be in the lounge at such a time, then told Concorde had been cancelled due to hydraulic problems. We were told that those who had to go home for work would get flown home by another plane, the rest could stay for two more days. I then hired a small aircraft to a small island. The story there was that in 1946 there was an earthquake at night all the fishermen at sea were drowned apart from one man. He swam towards the shore walked up the beach, saw cliffs facing him, walked back in and swam till he found another beach, this time he was in luck, found a house and knocked on the door, he was saved. We were told a lot of fishermen were lost. He was sent to

Cambridge to see how he survived that cold water. We flew back the next day, we were told you could have your money back or have another holiday, we opted for the holiday. That consisted of flying to Toronto, helicopter over the falls. I hired another plane to fly over the falls round CN Tower over our hotel, we then flew home by Concorde, the best flight I have ever had. Two weeks later going to work one morning the postman left a letter inside the money back. The story I have told you was for free.

MY HOLIDAY IN CHINA

It was a very interesting holiday but quite a bit scary for me. The reason was every day we went to a different place by coach, and I was on crutches. The bus stopped at its so-called destination. I asked our guide if the bus would stay put, he would say yes, we all got off, they followed our guide. I couldn't keep up, so I went my way, very interesting but scary, they would be missing for quite a while. I would head back to the bus in time for them to come back. I always took note where the bus was parked, when I found the spot where the bus was parked it was gone. I was very worried. Luckily, I found one of our group he put me in the right direction where it was. I went on board very happy. Eventually they all turned up. We then went back to where we came from.

A few days later, more sights to see. I went along as usual. The same thing, I asked our guide if the bus would stay put, the same answer luckily, he could speak good English. I wandered off on my own. No bus it had gone. I must have been stupid. I am lucky I am writing this story. It happened about four times. I don't know whose fault it was, the driver or the guide.

Then my luck changed, we visited the Forbidden City. I had a wheelchair, an ex-train driver pushed me around. We had an assistant guide with us. We wandered around we saw a lot of guides leading their groups holding something up so he wouldn't lose them.

My wife and the driver's wife, they got lost, made their way to the exit and waited for us. They met a woman that got lost going in.

We then went to see the terracotta soldiers, their horses, chariots, handy by wheelchair. My pusher had to rush to a toilet, that spoiled it a bit, another good trip. We then got off the boat at the end of our river trip, stayed in a hotel that night. Next day a trip to a vast zoo to see some pandas. What a disaster, stupid! . I went along, the bus pulled outside the main entrance. I insisted about the bus, same answer. I went with them as far as I could go. I left to go back to the bus, on the way back I stopped at a coach with the Yanks in. Stood outside, was an American I knew I said I'm going back to the coach can't stop, he said see you at our room as usual. I got within sight of where our bus should be: gone. I stood there sweating, thinking what to do. I thought my only chance was this American bus. I turned round and went back as quick as I could. There was this Yank stood there, I think he was expecting me. He went in the bus, came out with his guide, he told me to get in the bus. Off the bus left for the main entrance no bus, so drove back into a big car park in the zoo, found my coach with my wife in it. I am still here.

Next day we flew to a walled city on the edge of the desert. Flying there I looked out of a window. Down below I saw some pyramids they looked about the same sizes as those in Egypt. A fantastic view about six. We saw the city two ways out another interesting place.

We flew home from another good holiday.

MY NEXT HOLIDAY JAPAN

NO CRUTCHES

When you are there, you are in another world, there are so many places to see. The buildings, every one is different and marvellous to look at, people are the same, clothes and hats I'm writing this story from looking at these two photo albums all the pictures in colour. I can't find words to describe this country. I mention Nagasaki the damage the bomb did and Hiroshima and the memorial park the building, what's left of it still standing.

We then left Japan by our boat Spirit Oceanus to South Korea, about a day's journey to the port Ulsan Kyonggu a very big and busy place then went exploring saw Cheonmachong Tomb. As usual fantastic building to see and very well-dressed people. Then we went in an indoor market Kyonggu it was very big, all sorts of fish on display. After that had lunch and watched folk dancing Korean style in fantastic dress waving very flashy wands. We then went back to Japan by boat, our boat, then had a good look round Nagasaki saw the peace park, then sailed to Kyushu, the most southern Island of Japan, a volcanic mountain in the distance, has forests and grasslands, then another Island called Beppu on the eastern coast of Japan. I think that's all I have got to say about that holiday, time to go home back to everyday.

RUSSIA

We flew to ST PETERSBURG , known as the Venice of the North, the start of a month travelling the whole length of the Volga, first the explored ?Venice, travelled along some of the canals, interesting, saw two old sailing ships moored along the bank, we then came alongside an old three funnelled ship called the Aurora that fired blank shots to start the storming of the Winter Palace starting the October 1917 Revolution, it still looked in tip-top condition, then saw a very old looking schooner. Then, the next day we started visiting their museums. One showed you Rasputin sat at dinner table, they assassinated him. We visited about three museums: pictures, chandeliers, tables and chair in gold, all kinds of ornaments, money wasn't short in those days, it opened my eyes to the past. We paid a visit to the Yusupov Palace, the rooms full of decorated carpets, I could go on.

We then boarded our ship 110 passengers all crew, waiters, waitresses all Russian very friendly, food good not a thing wrong, then set sail. After about a day on the river we stopped off at a Transfiguration cathedral. It was made completely from different types of wood that would last for years. We went inside then visited Oshenov family house barn. We then moved on the next day, stopped off at Mandrogi. I called it a museum of traditional old Russian wooden houses, the craftsmanship was great, I haven't seen anything like it, photographs show the quality. Amongst this was a Vodka Museum. To top it all was Putin's summer home right on a lake, a walkway to the lake where he went fishing. I and Shirley stood in front of it twenty feet from the front door. It looked more like a bungalow to me. My opinion of the place and its value: every politician's house in Britain was worth a lot more. Next day we arrived at a church went inside, we were greeted by some monks, four all told, they sang to us all for nothing, but their voices, they made your hair stand on end, in my opinion I don't think there is anyone on this planet as good. Next day we stopped off at Goritsy Monastery one of the oldest and largest in North Russia. Next day we stopped off at Uglich we left the boat and wandered around, found an outdoor market, each stall was covered by a polythene sheet we were in a long time amongst trees. Most stall holders were women, very good looking, dressed in warm coats with fur collars, a very big woolly hat. We then moved on and found another building it could be a church don't know too good (?fore) that on top were these domes with a cross at their tops the colours were fantastic typical Russian. Inside more fantastic decor.

Then we left the Volga , went on a canal to Moscow and the Kremlin, wandered around exploring, had a good look at St. Basil's Cathedral in Red Square, took a good photo of it. Then we saw old Russian cannons on stands and just the barrels, then saw domes of the churches, then Cathedral of the Annunciation 1484-1489. Then we saw Tsar's Cannon 1586 massive to look at. Then a soldier came up to me out of the blue and asked if I would take a photograph before I realised there was about forty soldiers posing. I had a very good camera it did the trick wherever I went with my camera I never got stopped. I wandered off on my own. Nearby was a gigantic Tsar's Bell 1735 in its casting a big chunk came off well worth a look. We boarded our boat went back to the Volga.

Then we saw people dressed like cats. Then we saw this city Yaroslavl. This City stretches

18 Miles along the Volga. There was a lot to see. We had our breakfast in the boat at Pushkin. We then saw a mosque with the domes on top went inside and looked at the painting and

decoration great to look at. We wandered around a place which was old timber houses, small, felt roof. I wandered around with the camera as it was the first old place and run-down wooden fences with new car parks at their side. Later on, I saw a building under construction very high with arches at the top. On one side scaffold with two men laying bricks on the last arch. They stood at the very top with no handrail, that's never been allowed in Britain for years. We then stopped at an outdoor market, our next call was a lacquer factory, the very large eggs all painted I think it was the best factory in Russia. We then moved on to Kostroma, another place to wander around, saw a fantastic church with domes and a couple getting married, and an outdoor market.

Next day we arrived at Nizhny Novgorod. We then saw ladies dressed in fantastic clothes, dresses of all colours and jewellery, hats with beads all round, some with coins in bundles around their necks, ladies at stalls all dressed up what a sight. We then found a place with old Russian tanks, guns, planes, I think from the last war. Next place was Cheboksary, Kojan. At this place we came across a very large mosque, we then saw a priest, then a policeman, no black look about my camera.

The next port of call was Ulyanovsk, the birthplace of Lenin. Ulyanovsk, Gumbursk, with the same run-down buildings. The next place Samara there we saw a tall mast-like structure, and some very old trains. The next place Saratov was occupied by the Germans in the last war, there are still Germans remaining. We had a walk around the city. Next is Astrakhan the last place. I have photos of a wedding, bride and groom. This place was run down in quite a few buildings with oil pipes running from the desert. Now we leave our boat, we were told the plane could only take half of us home. We were told those that had to go back to work, they fly them home. the rest two days later would fly us to Moscow, a day there, then home, that meant two visits to the city. Next day we had a trip out in the desert, of we went by coach out of town, then we saw graveyards either side of the road. I have never seen so many gravestones, it was endless. Then I heard a man sat in front of us say when we are going to get to the airport, I thought he must be mad. I had seen him on the ship a few times with his wife. I thought this man (?) on a bus going to the airport with a woman and cases. So I called to our guide and told him that this chap is on the wrong bus, he went to the driver, we were going round an s-bend. I happened to look out of the window, saw a bus coming towards us. This bus stopped opposite, he got out walked across and went in. We carried on saw settlements with corrugated roofs, had their own patches fenced off. we arrived at a small settlement, we then got invited in this building. A group of women dressed in great clothing and hats. A priest with an unusual hat on, they entertained us by dancing and singing. It was worth going out to see them. We set off back to where we came from, we were then told this chap had caught the flight home. What a lucky man, we flew on to Moscow and then home.

OUR BONNIE TRIP

THE BUNIN SAILS OVER THE VOLGA

THE BUNIN SAILS OVER THE LAKES

WE'RE SAILING FROM ST PETE TO ASTRAKHAN

NO MATTER HOW LONG IT MAY TAKE

GREAT TOUR GREAT FRIENDS

REMEMBER THE CHURCHES MUSEUMS AND ALL

FOLK SONGS FOLK DANCE

THIS JOURNEY IS THE BEST OF ALL

YOU'VE CLIMBED EVERY STAIRCASE IN RUSSIA

YOU'VE SEEN EVERY FRESCO AND CHURCH

YOUV'VE SPENT ALL YOUR ROUBLES AND DOLLARS AND EUROS IN RUSSIA

FOUND BOXES AND ALL THAT YOU SEARCH

GREAT TOUR GREAT FRIENDS

REMEMBER THE CHURCHES MUSEUMS AND ALLL

FOLK SONGS FOLK DANCE

THIS JOUNEY'S THE BEST OF ALL

YOU'VE CHOSEN THE MENU AT DINNER

AND NEVER WERE SURE WHAT YOU'D GET

THE TEA PARTY AND RUSSIAN BLINY

THESE THINGS YOU WILL NEVER FORGET

GREAT TOUR GREAT FRIENDS

REMEMBER THE CHURCHES MUSEUMS AND ALL

FOLK SONGS FOLK DANCES

THIS JOURNEYS THE BEST OF ALL

The Hermitage Ranks the greatest

Museums

Louvre in Paris

London

New York

TURKEY

We landed on the coast, stayed in a very posh hotel, went swimming, wandered around, next day had a trip to Arena. Then next morning we boarded a bus with our cases and off we went not long before we were in a mountain range, it took all morning to get through them. We stopped at a small town had something to eat, we then set off. Nothing but flat land it could be a desert. All we could see was a mountain in the distance with snow on top. All afternoon in the desert we arrived at our destination about six pm. We were in for the biggest surprise of our life, the terrain was the opposite, you can't describe it. It was a massive V-shaped gully in rocks. On either side was caves by the hundreds where people lived in and are still doing so, houses in between them. In the foreground rocks shaped like mushrooms, much taller than the trees, at the top it overhung. I will try to describe them.: a cap on the top, the rock stem was softer than the top part. There was not one but many all over. I have never seen anything like it, that's this world, I wish I could have seen every bit of this planet.

We moved into our hotel, old but quaint and very smart. If you wanted to get up at 4am in the morning you could have had trip in a hot air balloon over the canyon with many more, I didn't bother, too early. I have had a trip in one close to home and I thought that was fantastic. You can see this happen on television advertising. In Turkey we saw them when we got up. I shall never forget this place and its sights. To top it all up, the night before we left, Shirley and Tom's wife and I went to see some belly dancing in a small hall, the dance floor wasn't very big either. I sat almost on the dance floor with my camera at the

56

ready, one lady kept coming up to camera very skimpy dressed, I got some very good shots.

Next day we set off for home, when I got back, I looked at photos very good. I thought a shot of dancer blown up would look very good, so I had six prints done. I took five to my golf club, gave one to each of my friends, the next time I saw them two brought them back they were told to by their wives. That's the end of this story

AZORES HOLIDAY OF 4 WEEKS

FLORES CORVO

GRACIOSA TERCERVA

SAO JORGE PICO

FARAL

SAO MIGUEL

SANTA MARA

The islands above are the islands Tom, Marge ,Shirley ,myself, paid them a whistle stop visit to. Very hectic, it turned out to be, but if you planned your life as we did it turned out a very good holiday and interesting. The four of us met at Heathrow, got on our plane to the main island and landed. Five minutes through the customs, seconds later I saw a person holding a board up with my name on it. She said follow me the four of us got in this four by four car, very flash, then off we went to our first hotel. It took very little time to get there, booked in a very smart hotel. She said be at the reception at nine in the morning then she left. We moved into our rooms settled in. then the four of us had a look round the town, then had a mid-day snack, later on our dinner. The food was very good, I thought if that's a starter, we are in for a good time. We had a chat, then we went to bed, got up early had breakfast then got ready for the day, camera and money, went to the reception early, there she was waiting for us. we went to the same car, and off we went touring this island all day. She stopped the car at all the beauty spots, we got out had a good look round and took photographs. We were told the name of the place this was, then we moved on to our next stop, had a mid-morning coffee, then a snack at dinner time, we travelled all day long seeing the sights, then headed back to our hotel in time for dinner. We were told to do the same in the morning, off we went to see the rest of the island. When we got back to our hotel we were told to be in the reception with our cases, then off we went to a small airfield no Customs, boarded a small plane, flew off to our next island. This happened with seven islands, fights twenty minutes or forty. two islands they were so near we went by boat and back. I have said enough about the travel.

What about the things we saw, small boats on jetties, the vegetation, bushes all over the place, plenty of flowers. we were told we were too early to see them in full bloom. They said some islands were covered in them. Wherever we went nothing was flat, lakes in sort of holes, greenery all around, the water was deep blue. I think they were created by volcanoes years gone by, probably thousands. None of these places were flat, very hilly mountains, When you looked down you could see the sea, and harbours, small towns at the back. The sky blue every day, weather perfect. On one lump of rock in the sea we saw a whale museum, outside was a mock whale about life size but in half. I don't think whaling is done now. (?) that was we had a real one day. Another island was nothing but volcanic rock, jet black, even the cliffs were black. All buildings were made from the same rock. Still, plenty of vegetation, even making small fields with black stone walls around for growing grapes. That island was much different from the rest. Another one had a volcanic eruption in 1940, we did get close up. A large town was annihilated ash all over. Nearby a lighthouse was buried in ash. The main building supporting it, doors, windows were underground. To sum up this holiday: lakes all the same shape, cliffs round the islands were spectacular. A photographer's paradise including the holiday. We flew home, shook hands all four of us.

Then problems started to happen then our luck in life ran out doctors hospitals every other week scans at Oxford very often Shirley was in trouble, she was recommended a treatment called CERTES back in Oxford after more scans she had the treatment told to come back in a month for the results. Four weeks later we turned up at this hospital we were told that it had spread and grown it was a cancer of the liver a doctor told us they would have a discussion and come back to us they never did-I rang this hospital at least a dozen times and my daughter doctor did at least ring four times I was in his surgery when he did, they have returned the call to neither of us. Thinking why this hasn't happened being it was research if it was a success, they would publish it in a paper a failure they didn't want to know. That's what I think. Anyway, Shirley's health went down very fast in a short time she was in hospital. For a while I was with her every day the last day they discharged her saying she could walk she came staying in our bed and not getting out going downhill very fast. The second week the chemist via the doctor suggested more medication that Friday I rang for an ambulance they took her to a hospice I followed with my night clothes. Nicola came back from Spain with the kids we both slept with her my bed six inches away from hers two days and one o'clock in the morning I heard her die my story ends now.

To continue my story

We went to Grantham in a car driven by Gary. My bag was jammed in the boot and in the back were his two sons and his wife. We had a long journey; traffic jams were continuous throughout our car ride. We finally arrived at our destination; my sister, her husband -and his parents were waiting for us. Then my cousin arrived to take me to my accommodation three doors away from the Thatchers' old home. I then booked in and paid the bill to get my keys. I walked four doors to my left, unpacked and did the usual.

Next morning things started to happen; we got into the car and travelled to Ancaster which was a village I spent my youth in. From what I remember it had changed a lot; the dance hall I spent my nights in had gone and two pubs I used to visit were renovated into restaurants. The road from the school to the railway station is now just a wild footpath. The left side of the path was an allotment, in my childhood where I used to grow vcg for the school dinners so the children could eat. In the village, I did not see any of the shops I used to wander around. Up in the north of the village I saw the house I first lived in which had not changed much. I did have a cousin four houses away and two cousins across the road when I was younger. Those houses too were still there but the malt kiln had gone. Further down into the village, we stopped near by a bungalow which I was told was where my cousin now lived. My cousin then welcomed us in and we had a long chat reminiscing about the past.

One evening, I was playing darts when a stranger came up to me and wondered whether I knew a certain person called Jim Gedney. The stranger himself had seen a farmer put five hundred pounds on him to win some time before the World War. I wondered how much that would be today. We then moved on to the church and graveyard, travelling around the gravestones finding many of them with the name Brickles. I took plenty of photos to prove they existed and now have printed many out. I had just realised that no Gedneys were living in Ancaster. They must have lived in a nearby village like Aisby which was where my Dad, his sister and Jim his brother were born. I had memories of spending my holidays there with my Grandma and Grandad. I shall go back next year and relive those moments from childhood.

This morning, Gary and his wife decided to take me back to Ancaster in his dad's car which I did not mind. He drove straight there. A quick drive around the village, then to the school I used to go to. It was very clean and smart: new windows and curtains were added from what I can remember. The school master's house was perched next to the school; it looked like someone was living there or it could be flats. We knocked on the door and wondered why none came to answer it. Spotting a person passing by, we asked if he knew who lived in the building, but he did not. A matter of time later, a car pulled up to the drive. Gary knew who he was once he arrived, it was the headmaster of another school. What was odd was that I used to go to the school almost every day until I was fifteen years old but never went inside the house. It turned out that Gary and his wife knew the headmaster's son and daughter as teachers in Dubai:.It was late and we needed our dinner. We ate our meal by the calming lake near the village. It dawned on me that at this very place when I was younger I saved someone from drowning one Sunday afternoon, but now its a safer, easier place to swim and be confident.

Next morning, I ate as usual and then sat waiting for my taxi driver to come and pick me up my friend Peter and me decided to travel to. We arrived at Aisby looking for my grandfather and grandmother's house. I did not recognised the village that had changed a lot but it did bring back many good memories.

I travelled miles for my gran so a doctor could see her: she was a hypochondriac. Or the numerous times I played football and won the championship for my team. We then travelled to another place which turned out to be a private estate. If I still remember my grandfather spent many long hard-working hours thatching, there with his son's wife as his assistant.

Grandfather thatching with his son's wife

Grandfather packing potatoes

From then on, we went on to Sleaford, a small town but a very well kept together place. We walked around trying to find the outdoor swimming pool and dance hall we spent our days in. It had changed a lot and I do not remember the town as it used to be. It looked a very nice place to live in, so my cousin said. We had a meal there and then set off back to Grantham, to see my brother and his wife. As luck turned out, they were in. We had a good chat as usual about our past. My brother did know Peter but just had not seen him for a while, he suggested a reunion.

Next day, we decided to visit all the villages that Gedneys had lived in in the past. We had little success but carried on, village after village. It was getting late so we headed back to Grantham and decided to have a late meal which was very good. I thought it would be ideal for the reunion the next day so we booked a table for ten and eventually everyone got there. The meal gradually arrived, and everyone was happy with what they were eating. There was a lot of talking between us all, with conversations about the living and the gone. Then out came the photos in all angles of which many have been printed. The place began to get empty which indicated us to leave one another for bedtime

Next morning, after breakfast I said my goodbyes to all. Peter left, Gary and his wife did and so it was my time too. I found my seat on the train, waving through the window taking in the experience I had. My daughter's boyfriend then met me at the station in London waiting for my next train to Reading. Through myself being late leaving Grantham, I managed to miss my train but in return I got a first-class carriage thanks to the assistant at the train station.

Thames Promenade at Caversham

We moved to Caversham to be near my daughter and grandchildren into a retirement apartment with fifty in the building, it looked very good, no garden, shops and bus stops ever so close by for Reading and other places to go to. After two years Shirley developed kidney cancer and the following year went to Oxford every two weeks for treatment but that failed, and she died a month later.

Then things did go wrong after the funeral, two weeks later I was on my own at night, so I decided to go to the lounge with trousers and shirt on to see the film show. The following afternoon I went to the working men's club close by and sat next to my friends, opposite was Wendy and Ray, then Wendy said to me 'I came inappropriately dressed to that' and then Wendy said it again in a loud voice that made me very angry. Another thing that happened to me, my cousin Peter from Grantham wanted to come to Reading for a week's holiday as he has never been to this place, he said he had two small dogs, I said ring around the hotels to see if they would have them, he then rang back and said that none would have them. Then I had a thought I would ask the new house Manager if he could keep the dogs in the guest room with them both, he, and his friend. She looked into this matter and said 'yes', they moved in for a week then hell broke loose, row after row at me, eventually I called for the top brass and he came and I called every one to be in the lounge at the same time, the row never stopped, eventually the brass produced a form to be filled in and I signed, that meant my cousin stayed in my room with the two dogs, his friend slept in the guest room. The rows didn't end, my cousin got fed up and left early, they will not come back again, the reason, dogs were allowed in only if you had a dog and wanted to buy an apartment, the new house Manager didn't know these rules, I have a lot more stories to tell, I don't want to bore you.

Then I didn't like the place and still don't, every morning after breakfast I got dressed and went out for a walk with a friend, I now do that every day since Shirley died. I have many pals in Caversham so I'm not that lonely during the day but at night I am, as I have my right foot amputated, I have to take it off at 5pm every night. Next day the usual walks, go different way so its not bored I think its Trevor, we might walk down the river to Tesco, we will decide when we meet up.

Over the years I have walked with different friends, the first person I have walked with was Viv and her dog, she told me about her 28 year old son, he got mixed up with drugs and drink, his mother and father had to go to court to sort him out, they then thought he had stopped, he got a job at Basingstoke for a month then the other Friday night came home and had a meal and a drink, the next morning the police found him dead on a bench, they think he took drugs. Three days ago I went to his funeral, I have never seen so many there, I asked his Father why, and he said most were his friends, I can see why, he was so good looking, another bad day.

Going back in time I started playing bowls out door, I was no good at it, but joined indoor bowls and was a lot better, that is where I met Trevor and become good friends. We walk most mornings as his wife was still teaching with a bad back. On our walks, I met a lot of people from Caversham, some have become good friends, and still are today.

In the afternoon I went to Costa for a coffee, becoming friendly with the staff, I have so many friends out and about it is fantastic, from the tales I have told you they make my life much happier. When the weather is wet, we decide to go into Reading for the morning, wander around the shops, bank and have a drink. If the rain has stopped, we walk home for our dinner, after that wash up and do odds jobs and then go out again.

About 3 years ago 1 went to Boots in Reading to see a friend I know, he wasn't there, a lady took his place I ask her where Paul was, she didn't know. I looked at he face and tears were there, I asked her what was wrong she said he husband had just committed suicide, I felt very sorry for her, lets go out and have a meal I will pay, from then on we became good friends, we see each other every three weeks.

Another chap came to live in one of our flats, I suggested we go on holiday, and we decided on Hayling island for a week, was very good weather. Another holiday was Swanage, my favourite place, went with my friend but the weather was not so good.

Freya, Ian
Hazel, Nicola

Time goes on, this coming week I am quite busy, hospital to sort hearing aids or a funeral. Now some good tales to tell, I have a daughter, she is a scientist, a 15 year old grand daughter who I think we take after her mother and another granddaughter aged 11, she went for a trial at football for the ladies team at Reading but didn't pass.

My 15 year old granddaughter wrote a letter to the new King asking him to get all nations to unite and stop fighting and for all the scientist to join up and invent new drugs so we could all live longer, and also all the scientist to unite and make better rockets to get further out in space and to get nations to stop chopping down the trees. Three weeks ago, I phoned my daughter and asked to speak to Hazel and she told me about the letter, so now will have to hope that he replies, my friend Gavin's son knew Freya at school.

I was chatting to a young lady and her dad wrote to the Queen as she was a horse rider, he did get a reply from the Queen.

My daughter is in London with Ian the boyfriend, every other weekend they do it, the girls are with their dad and that is usual. Yesterday I met three people from India by the river, one lady was on her own the other two were married, we had a long chat about the world and a good laugh, that was my day.

I think I have more stories to say about my life, I don't think it will change much.

I think I will put on hold any more words to say.

That's all for now.

Malcolm

Printed in Great Britain
by Amazon

26470149R00040